Dreams
of
Home ™

A Coloring Book for Grownups

Suits Sisters
Coloring Books ™

Coloring tips by the artists

The artwork in this book was designed to be colored with regular (hard) or pastel (soft) colored pencils. You can even combine the two.

Try using your pencil edge for shading while using the tip for hard lines.

Experiment with using more than one color in the larger spaces all the way down to the smallest details.

Leaving small bits of white space uncolored will add a luminous look to your finish art.

Pastels are extra fun because you can blend them with your finger tips to make the colors look soft and velvety.

Remember with pastels, you should spray a fixative on your final coloring to prevent smudging.

If you do want to try gel pens or paint instead of pencils, place a sheet of paper behind the drawing to prevent the color from bleeding through to the next page.

Find additional
Suits Sisters Coloring Books
www.SuitsSisters.com

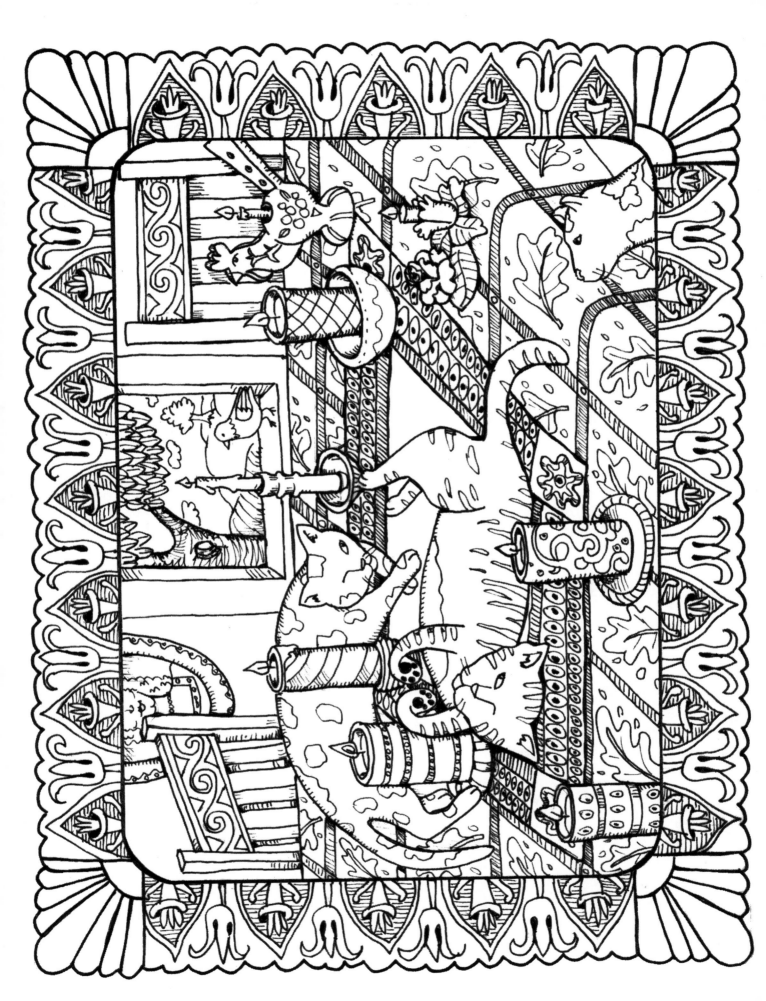

Artists' Bio

Helen and Thea are sisters separated by 2567 days and 588 miles. Born to working artists, they found their way somewhere in the middle of a mid-western family of seven. From paper to canvas and crayons to oil, art filled their senses. It was part of everyday life.

Taking different paths, Thea and Helen refined their talents, and over time they discovered their creative styles inspired and complemented each other. Today they find drawing together a natural and intuitive process.

"We had so much fun drawing the pictures for this coloring book. We hope you'll have as much fun coloring them!"

Helen and Thea

Contact the Suits Sisters:

Color@SuitsSisters.com - We would love to hear from you!

www.SuitsSisters.com

Suits Sisters
Coloring Books